BASKETBALL
in the Park

A Tribute of Gratitude To Our Fathers,

Roberto Baena Jaramillo
and Raymond J. Murphy

Text Copyright © 2024 by Gloria Baena and R.J. Murphy
Illustrations Copyright © 2024 by Juliana Castro
Cover Art and Design Copyright © 2024 by Juliana Castro

All rights reserved. No part of this publication may be reproduced, distributed, or transmitted in any form or by any means without written permission from the author, except for the inclusion of brief quotations in a review.

Permission should be addressed in writing to
Gloria Baena at gloriabaena2002@yahoo.com or to
R.J. Murphy at ray.murphy@arbjournal.com

First edition, 2024 / Design by Juliana Castro
The artwork of this book was rendered
digitally in Photoshop.
The text was set in InDesign.

This book can be purchased on Amazon.

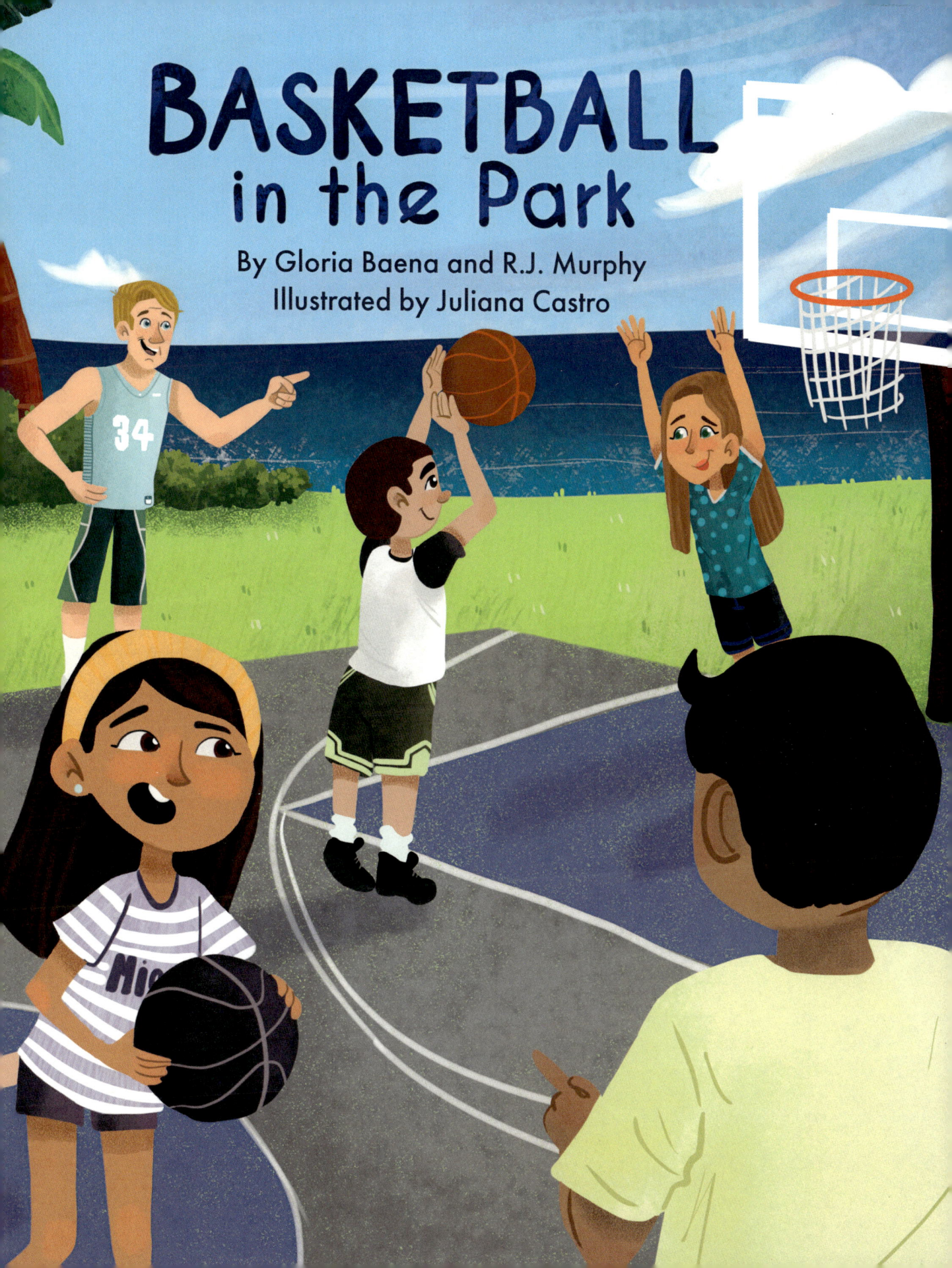

BASKETBALL in the Park

By Gloria Baena and R.J. Murphy

Illustrated by Juliana Castro

A few years ago, a man was working in Washington, D.C. He was a business professional and his name was Señor Murphy. He enjoyed his business life very much, but at times it became stressful. Thankfully, after business, the Señor had another passion: The Game of Basketball. He had enjoyed the game his whole life.

When Covid struck the world, Señor Murphy made a big decision to move to Florida in March 2020. The Señor believed that with the warm and pleasant weather he could be more productive, more healthy and more happy. Also, in his business life he had visited Miami many times and agreed when he heard from others that it is "The Magical City."

In Miami, Señor Murphy settled into his new home in the Edgewater neighborhood. He chose this location because it was on Biscayne Bay but also because it was right next to Pace Park, a beautiful outdoor space with a full basketball facility.

One afternoon in March, he was strolling through the park. After a busy day of work, Señor Murphy very much enjoyed visiting the park, especially the basketball court.

Basketball was certainly his passion, but sometimes he would feel sad because he did not have enough friends to form a team.

That afternoon, he noticed a group of youngsters playing basketball on the court — they were filled with joy and enthusiasm, but they also seemed a little unorganized.

Señor Murphy sat down to watch them play.

After a while, he invited the youngsters over and asked, "What are your names?"

One youngster responded, "Good afternoon, sir. My name is Marcela. My friends and I see you playing here all the time, but you always seem to be practicing alone and very seriously."

Señor Murphy chuckled warmly and said, "That is true. Sometimes it is important to practice alone, focusing on shooting, dribbling and other ways to improve. But you are right — basketball is best played with a team."

"But you still have not told me all your names."

I'm Charlie!

Felipe!

Danny

Jaime

One youngster said, "I'm Charlie, and the others are Felipe, Danny, Jaime, Andrea, Betty, Carolina and Marcela. We all live here near the park and have been friends for many years."

"Fantastic," said Señor Murphy.

Andrea

Betty

Carolina!

Marcela

Danny said, "Señor, you are very tall and strong. Is this important in basketball?"

"Excellent question," replied the Senor. "Yes, indeed. Being tall is helpful and having good physical habits is also very important. Practicing is critical. I was quite fortunate. My father and my coaches taught me all about basketball."

"By the way, do you kids have a coach?"

"No, we do not, but we would love to change that," said Andrea. "We have been a little frustrated and upset because we practice and try our best, but without a coach we have no technique and have lost many of our games."

"OK," said the Señor. "What do you think of me being your coach?"

"Yes," the group enthusiastically replied. "That would be our biggest wish."

"Fantastic," said the new coach.

Señor Murphy instructed the players to discuss the plan with their parents.

The players were told to promise that school and good behavior would always be the top priorities for the players.

Basketball would provide plenty of fun, but it also would require discipline, practice and training.

17

The next morning, after the players talked to their parents, the entire group gathered at the park for the first formal practice.

Señor Murphy explained that he had created a schedule and that he was motivated to see the team succeed. All parents and children were committed.

First, the new coach proposed that the team members agree to five rules:

1. Maintain good academic performance.

2. Respect the rules of basketball.

3. Respect all teammates.

4. Respect all other players.

5. Practice and play intensely but have fun.

Everyone agreed and enjoyed a delicious picnic. During the picnic, Señor Murphy asked the players a couple of questions.

"Who is your favorite basketball team?"

"THE HEAT," the players exclaimed in unison.

"Me too," said the coach. "That is a good start."

Jaime asked, "Coach, who is your favorite player and why?"

Señor Murphy paused to think. "Dr. James Naismith . . . because he was the great person who invented this wonderful game. He was a special man."

Then Coach Murphy had another question for the players. "What will your team name be for this season?"

The players were puzzled, as they had not thought at all about team names. Carolina asked, "Do you have any ideas, Coach?"

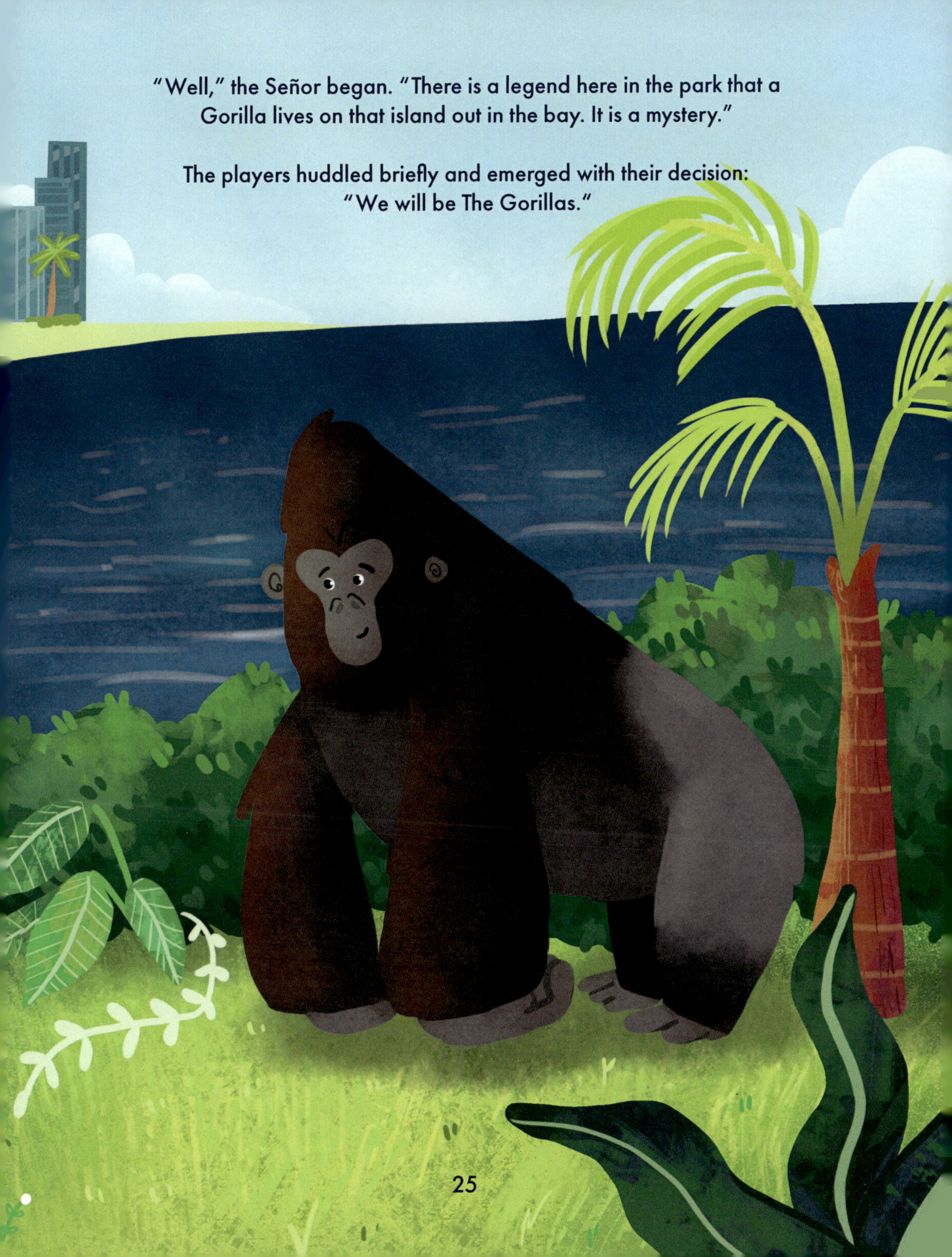

"Well," the Señor began. "There is a legend here in the park that a Gorilla lives on that island out in the bay. It is a mystery."

The players huddled briefly and emerged with their decision: "We will be The Gorillas."

With that, the team began its journey. As the season progressed,
the team attended practices diligently and settled into a training routine.

They patiently worked at improving in all parts of the game, with Señor Murphy
explaining the fundamentals of dribbling, passing, shooting,
rebounding and playing defense. The youngsters embraced their
new challenge.

After several weeks of practice, the team learned about an upcoming tournament to be hosted at Pace Park. Señor Murphy asked the youngsters if they felt ready for competition, and they all replied enthusiastically.

Andrea, Carolina, Betty and Marcela played in the first game.

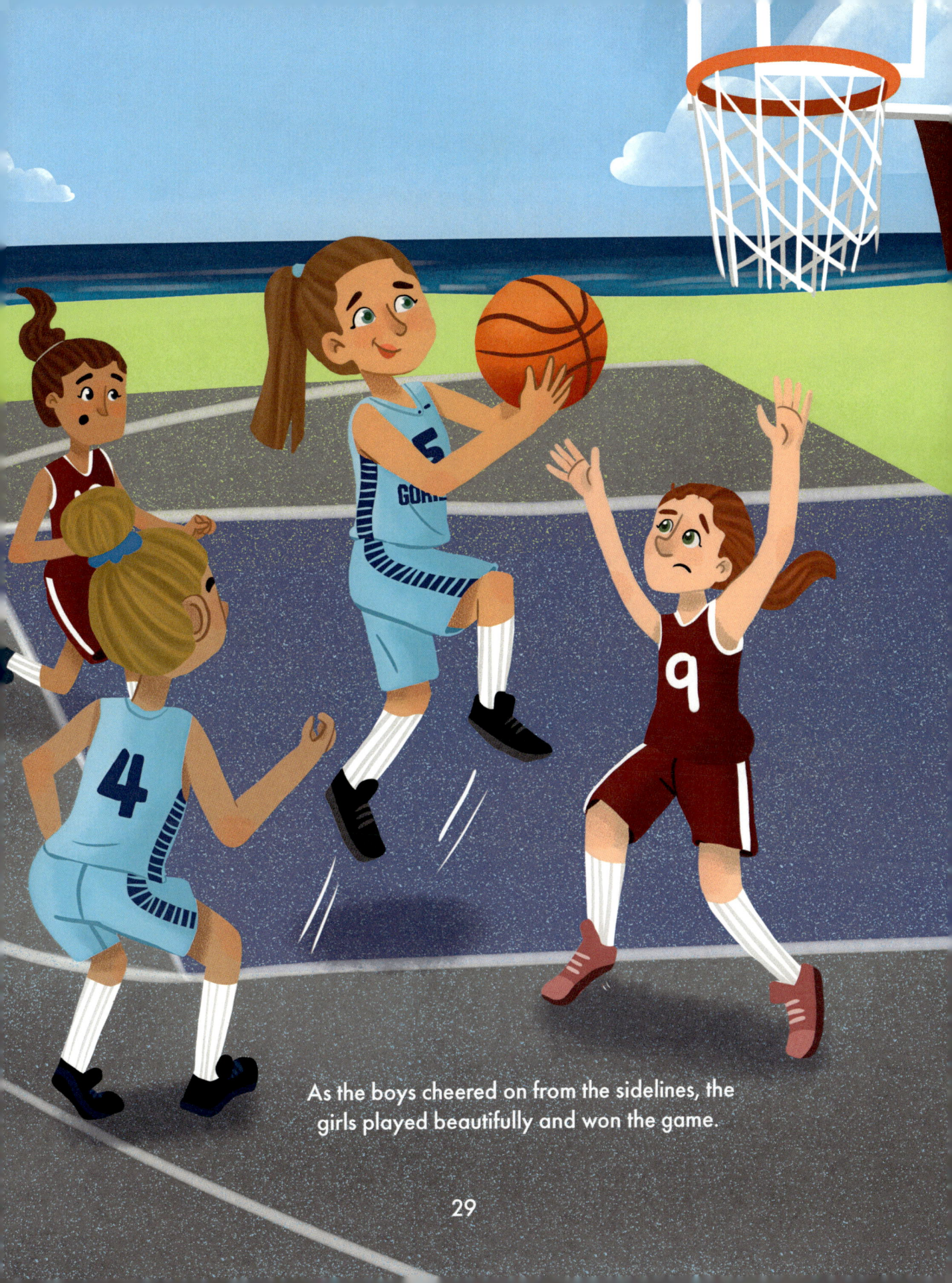

As the boys cheered on from the sidelines, the girls played beautifully and won the game.

35 − 28
GORILLAS — VISITORS

In the second game, Charlie, Felipe, Jaime and Danny also earned a victory, and all of the youngsters enjoyed a huge celebration.

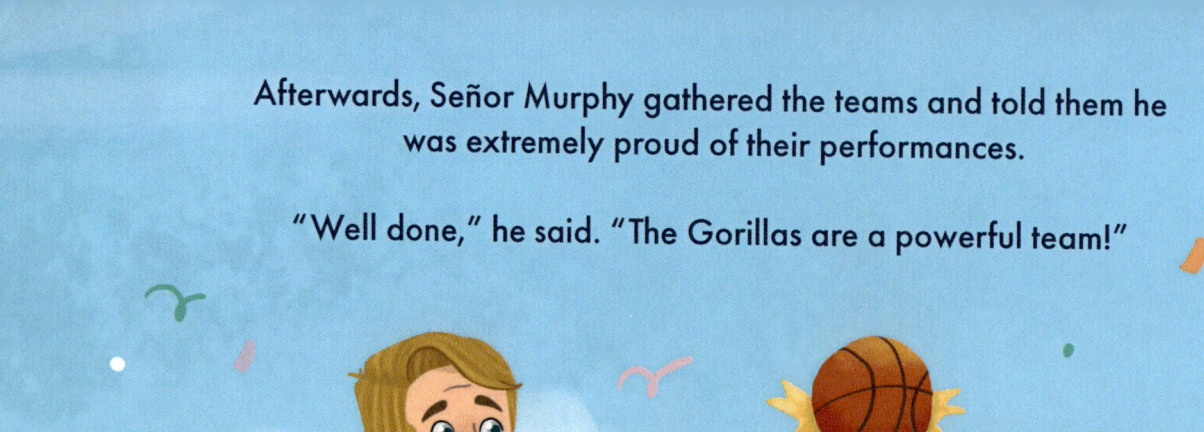

Afterwards, Señor Murphy gathered the teams and told them he was extremely proud of their performances.

"Well done," he said. "The Gorillas are a powerful team!"

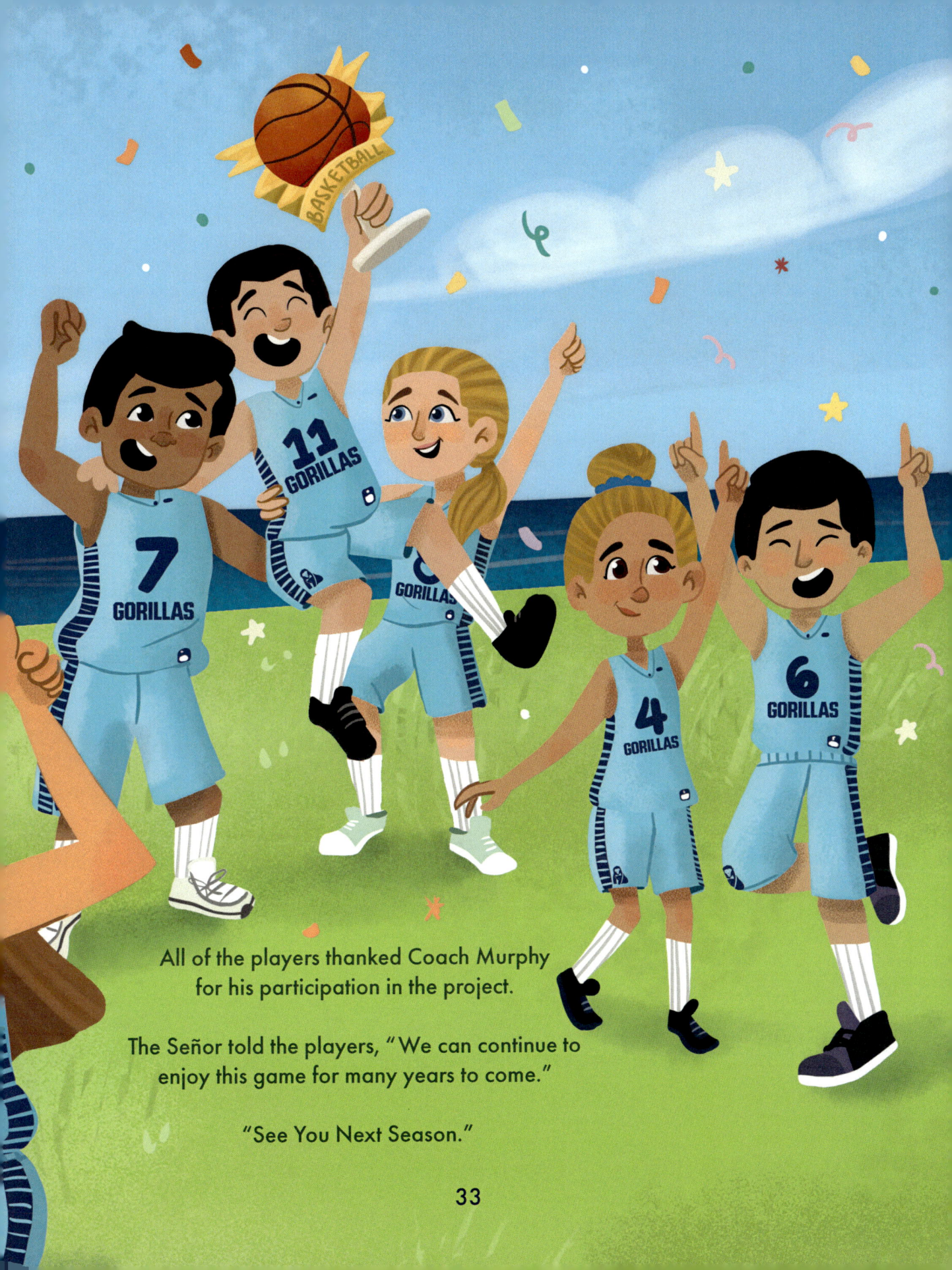

All of the players thanked Coach Murphy for his participation in the project.

The Señor told the players, "We can continue to enjoy this game for many years to come."

"See You Next Season."

About The Authors

Gloria Baena and her husband, R.J. Murphy, are writers based in Florida. They specialize in books and stories with positive and uplifting messages for children. Ms. Baena's previous books include "La Fiesta Del Gorila," "LA Busqueda," "Tito el Espantapajaros" and "La Granja," among others All books are available via Amazon.

About The Illustrator

Juliana Castro is a bilingual freelance illustrator from Bogota, Colombia. She creates story-driven digital and traditional illustrations for children's books, toys and games, stationery, and kids/tweens editorials. Her work mainly portrays animals, environments, and diverse characters. The purpose of her illustrations is to help raise awareness about endangered species, the beauty of nature, the environment, and Hispanic culture; all while bringing a smile to your face. She is based in Boca Raton, Florida.

https://julianacastrc.com/

Made in United States
Orlando, FL
06 July 2024